T0147666

Logic, Science, and God

Logic, Science, and God

How It All Fits Together

The Origin of Man's Intelligence and Our Destiny

PAUL STEVENS

iUniverse, Inc.
Bloomington

Logic, Science, and God
How It All Fits Together

Copyright © 2009, 2011 by Paul Stevens.

All rights reserved. No part of this book may be used or reproduced by any means, graphic, electronic, or mechanical, including photocopying, recording, taping or by any information storage retrieval system without the written permission of the publisher except in the case of brief quotations embodied in critical articles and reviews.

iUniverse books may be ordered through booksellers or by contacting:

iUniverse
1663 Liberty Drive
Bloomington, IN 47403
www.iuniverse.com
1-800-Authors (1-800-288-4677)

Because of the dynamic nature of the Internet, any web addresses or links contained in this book may have changed since publication and may no longer be valid. The views expressed in this work are solely those of the author and do not necessarily reflect the views of the publisher, and the publisher hereby disclaims any responsibility for them.

Any people depicted in stock imagery provided by Thinkstock are models, and such images are being used for illustrative purposes only.
Certain stock imagery © Thinkstock.

ISBN: 978-1-4620-3976-0 (sc)
ISBN: 978-1-4620-3977-7 (hc)
ISBN: 978-1-4620-3978-4 (ebk)

Library of Congress Control Number: 2011912855

Printed in the United States of America

iUniverse rev. date: 08/17/2011

Front Cover Photo Courtesy of NASA
http://www.nasa.gov/multimedia/imagegallery/image_feature_1168.html

To my wife, children, and grandchildren, Angela Zygaczenko, and Scott Pitcher who encouraged me to write this book

CONTENTS

Preface.. ix

Introduction.. xi

1. The Origin of Man... 1

2. Two Categories of Laws Governing the Universe
    and Man.. 8

3. Is There a Need for a God? 10

4. Darwin's Contribution 14

5. Evolution—True or False? Dogma versus Science and
    Logic 16

6. Lessons from a Bluebird.. 21

7. Learning Is Necessary to Progress and Be Happy 23

8. Can We Ever Know All There Is to Know? 25

9. Is the Bible Compatible with Science? 27

10.   What Does God Look Like? 30

11.   What Motivates God and Other Intelligent Entities to

Help Us? 32

12.   The Necessity of Experiencing Adversity, Death, Sorrow,

Pain and Suffering 34

13.   How God Administers Justice and Still Grants Mercy 36

14.   Mankind's Future 41

15.   How Can We Know for Sure? 44

16.   Logic, Science, and God—How It All Fits Together 51

17.   The Challenge 57

Notes 58

Preface

This project began seventy years ago when I was eight years old. Many childhood memories have diminished, but not the following event. I was having a conversation with a lineman working on a utility pole next to my home. The lineman said he was a minister in a local church and worked for the electric company to supplement his income. I told him which church I went to and that I believed what I was learning. He laughed and said, "Ignorant boy, the only reason you believe in what your church teaches is because your parents take you there and you don't know anything else."

Even though I was young, the comment made a great impression on me. I vowed to search for the truth aside from what I was taught by my parents. As I grew older, my search for truth led me to study the sciences and all the major religions around the world. I also immersed myself in the study of logic, epistemology (the study of how we know), philosophy, and the sciences from three major universities. The concepts I have learned have brought me understanding, contentment, and happiness. I desire to share these concepts with others to enjoy as I have.

Introduction

There is nothing more important in one's life than to be content and genuinely happy. We can be content and happy by learning and understanding the laws of nature and the laws of sociality and by living in accordance with them. Nonconformity to these laws ultimately results in misery and despair.

Logic, Science and God is intended to provoke thought and improve understanding for those willing to learn and adhere to the laws explained herein. The author explains through logic and simple scientific principles the truth about the origin of man, mankind's development, and how to obtain joy and happiness. The reader is encouraged to place the thoughts contained herein into the crucible of his or her own mind, analyze the material, and test it against well-established and proven principles. The author has drawn conclusions that, when understood, will bring peace of mind, knowledge of the origin and destiny of man, understanding, joy, contentment, and happiness, providing we live in accordance with the laws that govern us.

Chapter 1:

The Origin of Man

The Basic Laws of Physics

Since the dawn of time, man has wondered how mankind came to be. The answer is really quite simple. We must understand two basic laws of physics before we can understand man's origin. They are as follows:

First: The law of the conservation of energy, which states that matter can change form, but cannot be destroyed.

Second: Newton's third law of motion, which states that "*for every action there is an equal and opposite reaction.*"[1]

These laws are the basic laws of physics. We can draw sound conclusions from understanding them. One must rely totally on such unvarying laws in order to arrive at the truth about the origin of man.

From the law of the conservation of energy, we can conclude that matter has always existed—and will always exist—but its form can change when acted upon. Existing matter can never become nothing—and matter cannot be made from nothing as we can show with simple mathematics (0=0). *Nothing will always be nothing; and something will always be something.*

Conservation of Energy

We know matter has always existed because it cannot be made from nothing. We also observe that the form of matter can change in the same way that water does. Water can be in the form of a liquid, solid, or a vapor. *Matter can only be changed if acted upon*—otherwise matter would remain in the same state as it was before it was acted upon. What is it that causes matter to change its form? It can only be an entity with intelligence that has always existed like all matter does.

We shall define matter that can act and move upon other matter as an *Intelligent Entity*. Intelligent Entities have to exist or nothing in the universe could be acted upon to affect change. Matter only changes form when acted upon by an Intelligent Entity. There is no other way matter can change form. Obviously, something that can act could not have made itself, so reason tells us Intelligent Entities cannot be destroyed according to the law of the conservation of energy.

Action Is Necessary for Creation to Occur

In order for elements to be assembled or for matter to change its form, it must be acted upon by an Intelligent Entity that can cause action to occur; otherwise, matter would stay in its original state of existence. Sir Isaac Newton stated that "for every action, there is an equal and opposite reaction." The right actions by an Intelligent Entity cause matter to change form and creation to occur. Where there is no action, there can be no reaction or creation. There has to be an Intelligent Entity to act upon matter in order for any creation to occur.

The Origin of Intelligent Entities

We know an independent Intelligent Entity exists in each man and woman; otherwise, we would not be able to act independently of each other. Since nothing can exist unless it is made of something, we can conclude that the Intelligent Entity—though unseen—consists of matter.

Even though we are Intelligent Entities, we obviously did not make ourselves. Where did we and other Intelligent Entities come from? There are only three possible alternatives. *Intelligent Entities originated by chance, are made from scratch, or we have always existed. We shall examine each of these alternatives to see which one is correct.*

Did Intelligent Entities Originate by Chance?

Some may believe man's intelligence originated spontaneously by chance and evolved without outside intervention. *Chance is only a concept* and has no tangible, physical properties, is not composed of matter, and *cannot produce the necessary energy to cause creation to occur. Chance is composed of nothing. Nothing, such as chance, can cause any reaction to implement creation.* It takes something that can emit energy to cause reactions capable of causing creations to occur. Without action, there cannot be a reaction to cause creation. Chance is not part of the formula for the organization of matter. The intelligence of man could not have originated by chance.

Nothing Happens by Chance

If creations were made by chance, then Newton's third law of physics is not true. Instead, a law of physics would state something similar to the following:

> Creations are caused by chance. It does not take a thing that can act to cause creation to occur. Creations occur spontaneously without being acted upon by an outside force.

The above statement could not be a true law of physics because it takes an Intelligent Entity that can act to cause creation to occur.

What about Chance Occurrences?

We can clearly see that matter is organized only by an entity that can act, but what about chance occurrences? Don't accidents and other similar phenomena occur by chance? For example, two drivers in different cars collide at an intersection, causing an accident. Did this accident occur by chance? Let us examine accidents to see if they really occur by chance.

We have shown that an Intelligent Entity is the only thing that can organize matter or cause occurrences. Otherwise, things remain stagnant. We can then conclude that Intelligent Entities must be a factor in accidents or there would be no force to cause the accident. Therefore, there is no such thing as an accident that an Intelligent Entity is not involved in. For example, one driver is driving south and another is driving west. They collide at an intersection causing an accident. The accident was not caused by chance. The accident was actually caused by two Intelligent Entities setting in motion two different laws of physics that conflicted with each other.

Some may believe chance occurred when a driver willed a car to drive straight on a slippery, icy road. However, because of the ice—and against the driver's will—the car slid into a ditch, causing an accident. This can be construed to be a chance occurrence, but it is not. The real reason the accident occurred was because the driver's will to drive the car straight on an icy road conflicted with the icy conditions established by the laws of physics. Thus, the accident was not caused by chance, but by the will of a man conflicting with the laws of physics.

A tree branch suddenly falls to the ground, killing a person who was enjoying a picnic in a park. Is this an accident? The answer is no. The unfortunate person simply stood in the way of the laws of physics set in motion by an Intelligent Entity planting a tree long before the tree branch fell. It is simply a matter of the laws of physics doing its job over a period of time that was set in motion by the person planting the tree years earlier. The incident did not occur by chance.

Chance cannot cause anything to be created or made. All action in the universe is caused by Intelligent Entities using the natural law of physics. There is no phenomenon called chance that causes creations to be made or accidents to occur by themselves. What we call accidents only occur when the actions of an Intelligent Entity cause conflicts with the laws of nature.

Did a Big Bang Happen by Chance and Cause Man to Appear?

We may believe our universe was created from a big bang and that everything in the universe originated from the big bang, including mankind. We must remember that Intelligent Entities have always existed and it would take an Intelligent Entity to act in order to cause a big bang to occur. Scientists have often asked, "What was before the big bang?" They know something had to exist before the big bang occurred because nothing can be made from nothing (0=0). One thing is certain: Intelligent Entities have always existed and did not suddenly appear after a big bang. The big bang could not have occurred without action by an Intelligent Entity.

Were Intelligent Entities Made from Scratch?

Some may say Intelligent Entities were created and that no part of an Intelligent Entity existed before it was created, and that Intelligent Entities were created by God. They say God made man from scratch and that the intelligence of man did not exist before God made it.

Man's intelligence was *not* made by God from scratch for the reasons listed below:

A. *Mankind would be robots if our intelligence was created from scratch by God.* If mankind was totally made from scratch, including our Intelligent Entity, one must conclude that all men and women would be robots. God would have to program us in some manner or we could not function. Man

5

would only be able to act as he was programmed to act by God. Reason tells us nothing could have made our Intelligent Entity because we can and do act on our own, independent of all other Intelligent Entities. Therefore, our Intelligent Entity, whatever its composition, has always existed, or we would be robots. We all know we are responsible for our own decisions. We are not robots.

B. *Mankind would have no need for ethics if a man's Intelligent Entity was made from scratch.* We are taught right from wrong at an early age because we have the ability to choose between right and wrong independently, by ourselves. There would be no need for us to be taught right from wrong if we could not *choose* between right and wrong. Instead, we would have to respond exactly like God made us to respond. It would be unjust for God to punish us for something we did wrong if He programmed us to do it. We are free to choose right from wrong.

Have Intelligent Entities Always Existed?

Man's intelligence did not come into existence by chance or by being made from scratch. The only other reasonable alternative is that Intelligent Entities have always existed. We cannot see Intelligent Entities or know their composition, but we can calculate that they exist like other things we know exist that we cannot see, such as wind and air. All other possibilities for the origin of man's intelligence have been eliminated. We can soundly reason that Intelligent Entities have always existed independent of other Intelligent Entities, and that each Intelligent Entity can act on its own. An independent Intelligent Entity exists in every man and woman, enabling mankind to retain knowledge, make decisions, feel emotions, and act.

Since there is nothing known about the composition of Intelligent Entities, we can simply define it as a thing consisting of something, or we might possibly say it is composed of matter that

Logic, Science, and God

can never be created or destroyed, that can act and be acted upon. This is all we know in our current stage of existence. Because each of us is an Intelligent Entity, we are subject to the laws of the universe and can be acted upon by God and other Intelligent Entities.

Conclusion

Matter in the universe is in a state that can be acted upon by Intelligent Entities. What we call "chance occurrences," or accidents, do not happen by chance, but are caused by Intelligent Entities setting in motion conflicting natural laws of physics. All occurrences are the result of actions caused by Intelligent Entities. The idea that creations occur by chance is not based on science, any principle of physics, or sound logic and is not accurate. Creation cannot occur by chance. Creation only occurs when things that can act (Intelligent Entities) act upon various forms of matter. There is no other way a creation can be made. Nothing happens by chance. That mankind originated by chance relates more to a religious concept than to science.

We can be assured that man possesses an Intelligent Entity that has had a past without a beginning and will have a future without an end. Intelligent Entities have always existed, independent of each other, will always exist, and are an independent, intricate part of each man and woman. There is no other reasonable conclusion that can be drawn. If there have not always been Intelligent Entities that can act, nothing in the universe could have been set in motion, the universe would be stagnant, and Newton's third law of physics would not exist because there would be nothing in the universe to cause action to occur.

7

Chapter 2:

Two Categories of Laws Governing the Universe

and Man

The Laws of Physics (Natural Laws) and the Laws of Sociality

Reason tells us that the laws of physics governing nature must be obeyed for harmony to exist. The laws of physics were not made and cannot be made. They have always existed and will always exist. They can be counted on to never vary. Chaos can result when the laws of physics and nature are not adhered to. Harmony only results when these laws are obeyed. The laws of physics (natural law) benefit mankind when obeyed. They are a detriment to mankind if they are not obeyed.

The law of sociality concerns the treatment of others. They are actions of any kind that promote harmony among mankind. Any action caused by one person against another person that is harmful to that person in any way, whether physically or emotionally, would be breaking the laws of sociality. All action of one person toward another person must be for the benefit of that person. Any detrimental action willingly committed against another person constitutes a breach of the laws of sociality.

If every person strictly adhered to the laws of sociality, they would be conscious of the welfare of others. There would be no need for law enforcement. James Madison wisely said, "If men where angels, no government would be necessary." The actions of all persons would be in complete harmony with each other. Is it possible for man to evolve and reach such a state where everyone's actions conform to the laws of sociality? The answer is *yes!* Reason tells us that given sufficient time and desire, we can attain a state wherein all of our actions are for the benefit of others as well as ourselves. Before we can reach such a state, we must gain additional experience and become further enlightened. With additional experience and enlightenment, we can learn obedience to the laws of sociality by the things we suffer when we do not obey the laws of sociality.

Conclusion

There are laws of physics (natural laws) and laws of sociality. We must learn and obey all these laws in order to evolve into a higher state of happiness.

Chapter 3:

Is There a Need for a God?

Corporations have presidents, companies have managers or owners who manage their organizations, and countries have prime ministers, presidents, or other leaders. Reason tells us that every organization needs a leader—someone to direct, motivate, and help enforce rules and regulations for the benefit of everyone in the organization. Without a leader, an organization disintegrates, ceases to exist, or splits into different factions that then have leaders. The same applies to humanity in the universe. It is only reasonable that a leader must bring harmony to the universe and assist with man's progress—not just an ordinary leader, but an exceptional leader that knows everything and there is nothing save he knows it. If the leader did not know and control everything, something he did not know about could destroy us. An exceptional leader is essential in order to gain the confidence of followers. We need such a leader. It is obvious that we have our leader whom we shall call "God" who brings harmony to the universe and assists us in our progression.

Attributes a God Must Have to Be a God

A God must be all knowing, all powerful, just, and merciful in order to be a God. Our God possesses all of these attributes as explained below.

1. *God must be all-knowing.* There must be nothing save God knows it. We know this is possible because knowledge is finite concerning any matter, not infinite. The laws of the

universe must be completely understood for other Intelligent Entities, such as ourselves, to have total, unreserved confidence in him. Who would have confidence or faith in a leader that did not know how to control all laws—some of which could hurt us if not controlled?

No Intelligent Entity would want to rely on a leader who did not know all natural and social laws. We can reason that our God has conformed to all the rules for obtaining all knowledge. We can, with certainty, know that He knows everything, and there is nothing save He knows it and controls it. Man could not have evolved to where we are today unless our God knew everything, guided our evolution, and stabilized the universe so we can evolve.

2. *God must be all powerful (control all laws)*. God must have the ability to control all things. If there is something in the universe that He did not know about, it could destroy us. Our universe could be in a state of chaos. We can conclude that His knowledge gives Him the power to control all natural and social laws—and all variables and situations for man's benefit and the benefit of everything in the universe. He must live in conformity to all laws and know how to control them or he would not be all powerful. His power comes from understanding and living in conformity Himself with all natural laws and with the laws of sociality that have always existed.

3. *God must be just*. The laws of physics or natural laws are always consistent and predictable. They have always existed and will always exist. They never change and reason tells us that they never will change. We use them for our benefit. If we violate them or misuse them, they can be detrimental to us. In a sense, the laws of nature dispense justice. If obeyed, they justly reward us; if disobeyed, they justly punish us or give us no reward. There is no exception. It is exactly the same with the laws of sociality. If obeyed, we are justly

rewarded; if disobeyed, we justly suffer the consequences. There is no exception. If there were exceptions, order could not exist in the universe and chaos would result. All laws must be obeyed and justice dispensed. If we break any law, we must suffer the consequences. We learn obedience to laws by the things we suffer when we do not obey the laws. Justice must be administered and consequences suffered in order to have harmony in the universe so that man can evolve. Logic dictates this must be so. God must—and does—dispense justice in order to be a God.

4. *God must be merciful.* We know that the laws of physics or natural laws are rigid. They grant no mercy if violated. But, what about the laws of sociality? Can those who enforce the laws of sociality grant mercy to those violating the laws of sociality? Mercy cannot rob justice or there would be no justice. Justice has to be dispensed for order to prevail in the universe. We know that for every law of sociality that is broken, there must be a punishment affixed and enforced. Everyone would do what they wanted to do without fear of suffering the consequences if the laws of sociality were not enforced. Chaos would result. However, all of us have broken the laws of sociality at some time or another.

We must suffer the consequences of breaking laws. What are the consequences of violating the laws of sociality? It is reasonable to assume that we must be punished and possibly banished from a society where everyone obeys the laws of sociality. Why would those obeying all laws, living in peace, contentment, and happiness want to associate with those not obeying the laws and have their peace disrupted? The answer is that they would not. We have a parallel in our society. We put law violators in jail—away from law-abiding citizens. The same principles apply throughout the universe. The just do not live with the unjust.

For justice to be universal and fair to all, justice must be consistently implemented in every situation, with no variance.

Because none of us have obeyed all the laws of sociality, we must suffer the consequences of the laws we have broken. However, if we want to change and learn to consistently obey all laws, God would not be merciful if he did not prepare some way for us to escape the inevitable consequences that justice demands. The only way this can be done is to have the demands of justice fulfilled. It is crucial that all of us understand how we can escape the demands of justice. We have devoted chapter 13 to its explanation.

Conclusion

Every organization needs a leader to guide and direct, or chaos results. Reason dictates that we have such a leader in the universe or we could not have evolved into the state we are in today. Without a supreme leader (God), we would have remained in a state where we could not have evolved into a higher state of existence. Unless a supreme leader was present and willing to assist us, we would have remained an Intelligent Entity, in a dormant state, forever. We reason that God must be and is all knowing and all powerful. He can—and does—administer justice and mercy, and is willing to assist us or we would not be willing to follow him. We would not want him to be our God. Reason tells us that there *is absolutely a need for a supreme leader (God) or we would not be in the state of existence we are in today.*

Chapter 4:

Darwin's Contribution

Darwin wanted to know about the origin of the animal kingdom, among other things, and spend his life pursuing knowledge concerning such matters. Although many of his theories are unproven, some of his life's work stands.[2]

He discovered some scientific truths and theorized about others:

- A truth: Darwin contributed to reasons why the earth and prior life on earth is much older than 7,000 or 10,000 years old.
- A truth: survival of the fittest, or natural selection, occurs in nature.

The Age of the Earth

There is little doubt that the earth is much older than 7,000 to 10,000 years, according to the way we calculate years. Scientists now conclude that the earth may be from 4.5 billion years old to as old as 5.5 billion years old, which some say is contrary to the teachings of the Bible. (See chapter 9 in this book for Bible teachings concerning the creation of the earth and the meaning of days in the Bible.)

Survival of the Fittest, or Natural Selection

Darwin contributed to the understanding that the fittest animals survive the longest to perpetuate the species.

Conclusion

Darwin with other scientists have given us some insight into the concept of evolution and natural selection. Both conform to natural law. We must remember that Intelligent Entities have always existed in the universe. Intelligent Entities are the cause of all action we see in the universe, including the origination of species and their preservation. The method our organizers use to create and prorogate life on earth will become more apparent as our knowledge increases and our own evolution continues.

Chapter 5:

Evolution—True or False? Dogma versus Science

and Logic

The word evolution has many meanings. To some, it means that man evolved by chance to the state we are in today. To others, there is divine intervention involved with our evolution. Some do not believe in evolution at all, but others fear forming any opinion concerning the matter. First, we must define what evolution really means.

Definition of Evolution

Evolution is a process in which things change by degrees to a different state.

Evolution Is True

There is no question that evolution occurs. We see evolution occurring every day. Our knowledge is evolving every day. Society has evolved to what it is today. We have animals that are more varied and different than they were years ago along with many other examples. We can believe in evolution as long as we do not assume that evolution means it occurs by chance. There is a difference. Evolution must be caused by Intelligent Entities because nothing can happen by chance as we have shown in Chapter 1.

Conclusion

Evolution is obvious and occurs continually. The notion that man, animals, and plants originated by chance is contrary to the laws of physics (natural laws). Nothing can happen by chance, as we have previously shown. There are some conclusions concerning evolution that are false or are drawn from incorrect premises as shown below.

Dogmatism versus Science and Logic (An Example)

A wise man makes his own decisions; an ignorant man follows public opinion.
—Chinese Proverb

Definition of Dogmatic Statements. We will define dogmatic statements as statements, beliefs, or suppositions that are unsupported by fact at the time the statements are made. We should be careful not to form certitudes from such statements. Dogmatic statements of this nature are not always easily detected. Some statements are based on facts to begin with, but have faulty conclusions drawn from the facts.

One must determine if the premises to which the conclusions are based on are logical and based on proven scientific principles. If the statements are based on dogma or unproven statements, such statements should not be considered factual.

Deductive Reasoning. Examples of both good and bad deductive reasoning are given for the benefit of those readers who are not readily familiar with the more formal use of deduction. Sound deductive reasoning establishes sound premises before conclusions are made. Below are some examples of incorrect conclusions drawn with respect to death and the origination of man by chance or spontaneous generations.

Death as Incorrect Reasoning: Example One

I was listening to a lecture at a university by a doctor of philosophy who had been teaching at Stanford University. A flood had recently killed many people. He used the incident to talk about God. He exclaimed, "What kind of God would allow innocent people to be killed in such a flood?" He was inferring that God was not a good God. He was condemning God. The audience was silent for a long time as they contemplated the answer to the question.

As I thought about the question, it became apparent that his contention was not based on sound deductive reasoning. I stood and said, "Your condemnation of God is not based on fact. Your argument is based on the premise that death is evil. There is no evidence that death is evil. All men and women, whether good or bad, die. It is a fact of nature. You cannot say a fact of nature is evil." The professor, seeing that he had reasoned incorrectly, became embarrassed and quickly changed the subject. We know there is life after death as Intelligent Entities are eternal. It is imperative to think things through carefully if we are to assemble truths in our minds.

Origination of Man as Incorrect Reasoning: Example Two

First Premise: *The opinion of the majority of scientists concerning a matter can be relied upon as being true.*

Second Premise: *The majority of scientists agree that man ultimately originated by chance.*

Conclusion: Therefore, Man originated by chance.

The above conclusion is incorrect based on the above given premises as explained below:

Analysis of first premise: We know from history that the opinions of the majority of the people or scientists are not always factual. History shows that the opinions of scientists are constantly changing. Tomorrow's science will render today's science obsolete—except for proven basic principles that can be replicated time after time.

The first premise is false. "The opinion of the majority of scientists concerning a matter can be relied upon as being accurate."

Second premise: The majority of scientists agree that man ultimately originated by chance.

Analysis of second premise: It is a dogmatic statement to say the majority of scientists agree that man originated by chance. There are no known published surveys showing that the majority of scientists agree "man originated by chance or was spontaneously generated." Obviously, the second premise cannot be relied upon as a true statement without reliable surveys being conducted. Most of the scientists the author is acquainted with do not believe man originated by chance.

There is no evidence the *majority* of scientists agree that man ultimately originated by chance.

Correct Reasoning

The conclusion that man originated by chance is not a conclusion to be drawn from the two premises.

Evolution does occur and is a sound true principle in which things change by degrees to a different state. There is no evidence that the majority of scientists agree that man originated by chance. We must draw conclusions only from sound deductive logic based on proven scientific principles. We should always determine if statements are based on sound logic and proven scientific principles before forming certitudes. If our certitudes are incorrect, our mind

Paul Stevens

blocks out thoughts containing truths that are necessary for our learning and progression. Evolution does occur, but to conclude that man originated by chance or by spontaneous generation is not scientifically sound—and it is not correct.

Chapter 6:

Lessons from a Bluebird

Some minds are like concrete—all mixed up and permanently set.
—Anonymous

Early one Sunday morning, a terrible thud on our living room window woke me up. While I was figuring out what it was, I heard the sound again. I went to investigate the matter, but could see nothing that would cause such a loud noise. I did observe a big moth flying against the window trying to get out, but nothing that would create the loud noise I kept hearing. Suddenly, I saw a large bluebird dart from a nearby tree and slam into the window with great force. The moth was on the inside of the window. The stunned bluebird returned to the same branch on the tree. It waited for several minutes with its eyes fixed intently on the moth. Somewhat recovered, the bluebird again hit the window, hoping to make the moth its next meal.

I began to wonder how long the bluebird would continue slamming into the window before it understood there was a barrier separating them. I decided to wait and see how many times the bluebird would continue its attempt to eat the big moth. Much to my surprise, the bluebird continued to hit the window, time after time, until i could see it was losing its strength.Suddenly, the moth flew to another place in the room where it couldn't be seen by the bluebird. The bluebird continued to sit on the same tree branch, perched and ready for action, hoping to see the moth again. The bluebird never got its meal.

Paul Stevens

Conclusion

Some people are like the bluebird. They desperately try to make their idea work—no matter what. They refuse to admit that their ideas may be wrong. Man cannot arrive at the truth and progress by being stubborn and unwilling to change. Every concept, whether it is a scientific concept or a religious concept, must be approached with an open mind. A person must be willing to change their mind and admit that they may have been wrong—no matter what the consequences are.

Chapter 7:

Learning Is Necessary to Progress and Be Happy

Ivan and Yuri

Reason tells us that it is necessary for man to learn the laws of nature and sociality and live in conformity with those laws in order to progress or evolve into a higher state of existence and happiness. One cannot use laws if the laws are not understood. It is also easy to break a law, to our detriment, if we do not know it exists. Knowledge always comes from without. Knowledge never comes from within and then only by invitation.

The story is told of two young men, Ivan and Yuri, who lived in Russia many years ago. Ivan tried to learn all he could and Yuri only tried to get by. They both graduated from school at the same time. Both youths were hired by a well-known merchant living on a hill in a small Russian town. They started working together at the same time for the same hourly wage.

After a year, Ivan was given a large wage increase while Yuri received no wage increase at all. Yuri was very upset and complained to the merchant about it. The merchant, desiring to explain why, called both boys together and pointed to a loaded wagon that was just coming into town. He asked Yuri to run down and see what was in the wagon. Wanting to be a good employee, Yuri quickly ran down the hill to the wagon. He soon came back and reported to the merchant that the wagon was carrying a load of wheat. The merchant thanked him and then asked Ivan to go down and see what was in the wagon. Ivan took much longer to return. He then explained that the man driving the wagon wanted to sell the wheat for a lower price than usual. He said that he had inspected the wheat and found it was very clean, had no weevil, was dry, and could be stored easily. Ivan also said the wheat had come from a nearby town known to have wheat high in protein. Ivan concluded by saying there were five other wagonloads of wheat the farmer would sell at a good price, and he would deliver the wheat for free. The merchant then turned to Yuri and said, "Do you now know why Ivan received a raise and you didn't?"

Yuri understood and vowed to be more diligent. Like Yuri, we can get by and be complacent or we can be like Ivan, eager to learn and progress. *No one can progress in ignorance.* We only learn if we seek to learn. The more we learn, the faster we progress.

It does not matter how much knowledge is available to us if we do not diligently seek to learn and understand. There is simply no way we can progress and evolve into a higher state of happiness without learning and becoming willing to live according to the truths we have learned. Gaining knowledge is an essential part of the formula for being content, joyful, and happy. We can evolve into a higher state in the shortest period of time by learning as much as we can at present. We must simply learn about the laws of nature and sociality and live in conformity with them in order to progress. Unless we progress, we regress.

Conclusion

We must always seek learning and have the will to live in conformity with the laws we gain knowledge of, in order to evolve into a higher state of existence and happiness. Man cannot progress remaining in ignorance. We cannot evolve any faster than we gain understanding and knowledge of laws, appreciate them, and are willing to live in accordance with them. Knowledge, by itself, does not bring happiness. It is obvious that we must learn and live in accordance with all laws in order to progress and be truly content and happy.

Chapter 8:

Can We Ever Know All There Is to Know?

Knowledge is an intricate part of the formula for creation, as we have shown. *Nothing can be made without the knowledge to make it.* Things that can act (Intelligent Entities) must possess the necessary knowledge to organize anything properly.

We must say that knowledge must be finite with respect to any creation. We can clarify that statement by using an example of an architect preparing plans for a home to be constructed. The architect must know about the different components he wishes to have in the home before the home can be built. For example, if the architect did not know about plumbing, the home could not be built as a modern, livable home. There is a finite amount of knowledge necessary to be able to draw home plans so a modern, livable home can be constructed. The same principle applies to anything made in the universe. A universe could not have been created unless the creator knew all about how to make a universe. Also, any creation could possibly be destroyed by some occurrence if the Intelligent Entity making the creation did not know about—and have the ability to control—all possible variables.

Knowledge is accumulated gradually, a little at a time. Man has not obtained sufficient knowledge to create a universe by any means. However, if we continue to learn and obtain sufficient knowledge, it is logical, given time, that we may be able to create a universe. This can only occur if we learn about all the laws, live according to all laws, and use the laws correctly. As we have shown, intelligent entities have always existed and will always exist without end. Therefore, we have time to learn all there is to know if we are obedient to all the laws and our governing Intelligent Entity trusts us to always be obedient.

Conclusion

It takes a finite amount of knowledge to create something—not an infinite amount. However, nothing can be created or made without the knowledge to make it. The universe could not have been made by chance—it had to have been created by an Intelligent Entity or entities possessing finite or omniscient knowledge concerning the making of universes. We can also see that given sufficient time and knowledge, it is conceivable that enough knowledge can be accumulated by man to become omniscient if it is the will of the governing Intelligent Entities. There is no reason for the governing Intelligent Entities to restrict our learning if we are willing to obey the laws of nature and the laws of sociality. Realizing this, and given a long period of time, there is no limit to what man can learn and accomplish until he reaches the state of omniscience where everything to be known becomes known. It is not logical to think there is a cap or a restriction on learning.

Chapter 9:

Is the Bible Compatible with Science?

We can easily draw faulty conclusions by relying on the interpretations of others concerning the Bible.[3] We must read the Bible to determine if its teachings are true and compatible with the laws of sociality. We can trust ourselves to interpret the Bible correctly if we follow the directions in chapter 15, which show us how we can really know for sure.

The Bible's greatest contribution is in its teachings concerning mankind's relationship to God, our leader. We need to understand and live by these teachings if we are to evolve into a greater state of happiness.

The Bible addresses a great variety of topics, including the origin of the earth, historical events, ethical teachings, God's attributes, and future events. Let us review each of these topics separately.

1. **Origin of the earth.** One could say that the Book of Genesis in the Bible is illogical when it states that the earth was made in seven days, but if seven days means seven time periods, it makes sense. Seven days in the Bible must be interpreted to mean seven time periods—then it is compatible with science.

   The sequence of events concerning the creation, as explained in Genesis, corresponds with the present scientific view of the events of earth's creations. The only question is whether a day means a period of time or twenty-four hours. It is only logical that it means a period of time. We must use common sense when reading the Bible. In summary, the Bible supports scientific views concerning the origin of the earth when we realize that seven days means seven time periods. It defies all logic to think that the earth was formed in seven twenty-four-hour time periods.

2. **Historical events.** Scientists use the Bible when studying areas referred to in the Bible. Scientists would not use the Bible if it did not assist them in their research. Scientists find much evidence in their research that supports the events referred to in the Bible. Some say certain Biblical events did not occur because there is no evidence that they did occur. Such a conclusion is not based on good deductive logic. Just because there is no evidence to date that an event occurred, it does not mean that the event did *not* occur. To think such, one would have to erroneously conclude that all the evidence discovered today is all the evidence there is or will ever be discovered. We all know tomorrow's science can render today's science obsolete. It is not important that we know today what may be discovered tomorrow because it does not affect our evolution toward greater happiness. Absence of evidence is not evidence absent.

3. **Ethical teachings.** Few will dispute the ethical teachings of the Bible. They are teachings that all mankind would be well to conform to. The Bible's ethical teachings correspond to the known laws of sociality. All mankind must observe the laws of sociality if we are to live in harmony in the universe. The Bible is a reference source for ethical teachings and must be revered and studied. The standards set forth therein must be observed if we are to be content and happy.

4. **God's attributes.** It should be clear to everyone that it is necessary to worship something that actually exists. It would do no good to worship the sun, moon, or inanimate objects that have no power to respond to the worshiper. A true God must be alive, animated, and able to respond to the

inquiries of His worshipers. God must have the knowledge to control events in the universe. No other God would be worth worshiping. We will describe what God actually looks like in chapter 10.

5. **Biblical prophesies.** Early in this century, the Bible's prediction seemed improbable when stating that the Jews would return to Jerusalem, and build up a country in a bleak desert already inhabited by others. The Bible's prediction that the Jews would return to Jerusalem caused many to doubt the truth of the Bible. To many people's amazement, the Jews did return to the area. It is clear that many of the Bible's prophesies have been fulfilled, which lends credence to biblical prophesies.

Conclusion

Although the Bible addresses several topics, it is essential to understand that the Bible's ethical teachings are at the core of things to consider. Its teachings are logical. If we obey them, we will evolve and progress to greater understanding and happiness. The ethical teachings of the Bible conform to the laws of sociality and are absolutely essential for us to understand and obey if we are to free ourselves of guilt-and progress toward greater understanding, happiness, and contentment.

We can conclude that the Bible's teachings complement science and logic and they are especially helpful in understanding the laws of sociality that we must all obey to be happy.

Chapter 10:

What Does God Look Like?

There are those who think that God is a nebulous entity. There are many various beliefs concerning the nature of God. Most descriptions of God have been concocted by men wanting him to be like they want him to be. Because the Bible is compatible with science, we will use the Bible to discover what God looks like. We can certainly conclude that God is composed of some kind of matter, or he could not exist. The question is what does God look like?

If we discard man's commentaries concerning God and go directly to the Bible for the answer, we find the Bible describes God as being manlike in form.

The Bible Describes God as Being Manlike in Form

- We are made in the image of God, according to Genesis 1:26-27. "And God said, Let us make man in our image, after our *likeness*: . . . so God created man in his own image, in the image of God created he him; male and female created he them." If we are made in his image, then God must be manlike in form as we are.

- After Jesus died, He took up his body and showed himself several times to others in manlike form. One example is when Jesus showed himself to the apostle, John the Beloved, on the isle of Patmos. John described Jesus (the Son of Man) as a most glorious being when he said he was "clothed with a garment down to the foot, and girt about the paps with a golden girdle. *His head and his hairs were white like wool, as white as snow; and his eyes were as a flame of fire; And his feet like unto fine brass, as if they burned in a furnace; and his voice as the sound of many waters . . . and his countenance was as the sun shineth in his strength"* (Revelations 1:13-16). What a marvelous being. If Jesus has a body as John described, surely his father (God) must have a body also. A son cannot be the son of a father and not have the same type of body as his father.

The above is a description of a most marvelous being. Jesus Christ said, "I speak that which I have seen with my Father, and ye do that which ye have seen with your father" (St. John 8:38). This shows that He learned from His father as we do from our fathers. Furthermore, he was sent by his Father as He said, "And we have seen and do testify that the Father sent the Son to be the Savior of the world" (St. John 4:14). We see Jesus did the bidding of his Father and what son does not have a body similar to his father's?

We also know that God the Father is a separate person because Jesus prayed to His Father many times. It is not reasonable to think Jesus would pray to himself. This is further evidence that God the Father and Jesus Christ are separate anthropomorphic beings.

It is logical to think that God is able to talk to us and hear us. He could not govern us if He could not communicate with us and hear us. What mysterious force that cannot hear—or talk—could possibly be our God and govern us? There is no such phantom force.

Conclusion

It is reasonable to conclude that the Bible is correct when describing both God and Jesus Christ as possessing perfect glorified incorruptible bodies that are manlike in form. There is no other logical way to describe God. God is not a phantom.

Chapter 11:

What Motivates God and Other Intelligent Entities to Help Us?

Love Is the Motivating Factor

Why would God want to pay attention to us personally? The reason is simple. He loves all of us. When we help others, we feel good. It is the same with our God. The more individuals God assists, the happier He is.

We might say that there is a law in the universe, which could possibly state, "For every *good* action, there is an opposite and equal *good* reaction." Realizing this, we can understand why God and other intelligent entities would want to assist us. Good action brings affection, tenderness, and other good emotions to us, which we shall define as "love." We can clearly say that love brings happiness and is something God and everyone understands.

Like our Heavenly Father, we must love others. He has advised us to "love our neighbors as ourselves" (Matt. 22:39). We must desire to love and be loved. Love affects all Intelligent Entities—just as the laws of physics and the laws of sociality affect us. To love and be loved is one of the most sought-after emotions. It is something that comes into our lives by invitation only. Love does not come into our lives uninvited. We desire and *will* to love and be loved—or we will not experience love.

Love is not limited to any amount. The feeling of love can expand and grow. By endlessly expanding our love—by helping and loving many people—we endlessly expand our happiness. Our God understands this principle and implements it.

There are many ways we can expand our love. Some examples of how we expand our love are when we are empathetic toward others, practice long suffering, are kind, helpful, unselfish, slow to be provoked, and are willing to serve others. The more we love, the greater the pleasure, joy, and happiness we possess. To be happy and have joy is the ultimate goal of our God and for all of us.

Love is the great motivating factor for God and other intelligent entities to assist us in our evolution. There would be no motivation for God—or any other Intelligent Entity—to assist us if love did not motivate them to do so. We would simply not be able to progress without the assistance of God and others who are motivated by love to assist us.

Conclusion

Love is a willed phenomenon that can be expanded endlessly. Love brings happiness and joy to our God when assisting us to attain joy and happiness. Love is what motivates God to assist us in our evolution.

Chapter 12:

The Necessity of Experiencing Adversity, Death,

Sorrow, Pain and Suffering

I was visiting a man who had severe rheumatoid arthritis; his hands were severely deformed, and he could hardly walk. When our conversation turned to his condition, he said, "What kind of God would do this to someone?" He showed me the terrible condition of his warped hands and crippled feet. "I don't believe in God because a God wouldn't make someone suffer like this!" His condition caused me to seriously reflect. I concluded that there is a good reason why God would allow this man—and many others in the world—to suffer in such a manner.

In life, we all suffer in some way—whether it is financially, mentally, physically, emotionally, or in some other way. The question is, "Why?" We see others seemingly glide through life without suffering adversity, without realizing that they too, some time in their life, have suffered—or will suffer—adversity in some manner. Although unpleasant, we all need to experience adversity, guilt, sorrow, and pain. This is part of our learning experience. We would not value life without pain and sickness and other forms of adversity unless we experience pain, sickness, and adversity ourselves.

> It is not good for all our wishes to be filled; through sickness
> we recognize the value of health; through evil, the value of
> good; through hunger, the value of food; through exertion,
> the value of rest.
> —Greek proverb

34

Why death? We would not appreciate life that never ends without experiencing life that does end. We would not appreciate loved ones as much unless we experienced life without loved ones for a time.

We also learn by seeing the adversity others experience. It is not necessary for us to experience each form of adversity personally. We experience adversity when we see and witness the pain, suffering, and sorrow of others. Adversity exists for all of us to experience, whether by ourselves or vicariously through the experience of others.

We also learn obedience by the things we suffer, otherwise we would be content and not change. We seek God's help when we experience adversity. If we don't seek him, he cannot help us. We must seek his advice if we are to grow and progress. Adversity causes us to seek God for help.

Conclusion

Experiencing adversity is part of our earthly learning experience. We cannot be thankful and appreciate the absence of death, guilt, sorrow, adversity, pain, and suffering if we have not experienced such things vicariously or through others. Without experiencing adversity, we cannot appreciate its absence. Various kinds of adversity are absolutely necessary for us to experience by ourselves or by witnessing it in the lives of others if we are to have empathy towards others and become thankful when not experiencing adversity.

Chapter 13:

How God Administers Justice and Still Grants

Mercy

Justice

We use laws of physics (natural laws) for our benefit. If we violate them or misuse them, they become detrimental to us. In a sense, the laws of physics always dispense justice. If obeyed, they always justly reward us. If disobeyed, they always justly punish us. There is no exception. It is the same with the laws of sociality. If obeyed, we are always justly rewarded; if disobeyed, we are always justly punished. There is no exception. If there were exceptions, order could not exist in the universe, and chaos would result. If we break any law, we must suffer the consequences of breaking that law.

> Justice is a contract of expediency, entered upon to prevent
> men harming or being harmed.
> —Epicurus

Mercy

The laws of physics, or natural laws, and the laws of sociality grant no mercy if violated. But, can mercy rob justice? No, justice must be dispensed at all costs or order cannot prevail in the universe. All of us have broken natural and social laws and suffered the consequences. Justice is usually dispensed immediately when we violate natural laws, but it is not always the case when we violate the laws of sociality. There is often a time between when we violate the laws of sociality and the time justice is dispensed. We should be most grateful this is the case. It gives us time to seek forgiveness and mercy. If we have violated a law of sociality and have not yet suffered the consequences, we then have two choices. (1) We can attempt to avoid suffering the consequences of the violation by ceasing to further violate the law and plead for forgiveness and mercy to escape punishment from those administering justice, or (2) we can simply wait for justice to be administered and suffer the consequences personally. These are our only two choices.

How to Plead for Forgiveness and Mercy

It is not easy to obtain mercy. We must follow strict procedures. The procedures we must follow are as follows:

First. We must be sorry for what we have done and learn not to repeat the offense. We must try to make restitution where applicable.

Second. We must become teachable. We must be willing to learn and not think we know it all. We must cease trying to make God out to be what we want Him to be instead of accepting Him as He really is, our judge. Even though God loves us, God must always strictly enforce the laws of sociality and administer punishment for violating such laws. If not, God would cease to be a God and chaos would result in the universe.

It is well known among psychologists that *our moral behavior determines what we believe in. Only when we want to change our moral behavior, will we change our beliefs.* Unless we are careful, it is easy to discard truth because it does not conform to our beliefs, or it conflicts with the way of life we are comfortable with living. Unless we humble ourselves and are willing to learn to accept truth as it really is, and live accordingly, we cannot be forgiven and receive mercy. We must suffer the inevitable consequences of violating the laws and suffer, which suffering can be sore, and exquisitely sensitive, when all our wrong deeds become known. It will be hard to bear.

We will all eventually learn to live according to all the laws because we suffer when we do not obey laws, and will become tired and weary of suffering. We learn obedience by the things we suffer. We will want to change. If we are willing to learn and be teachable now, we will be eligible for mercy to intervene so we can avoid the suffering that is the inevitable consequence of justice being administered.

Justification for Mercy

How is it that God can grant mercy without robbing justice? In order to have perfect order in a society where ultimate happiness abounds, it is imperative that justice is rigidly enforced for every violation. However, the demands of justice can be fulfilled if another party is willing to intervene and pay the price to fulfill the demands of justice. A simple example would be if a daughter was fined for violating a traffic law. The father, who loved the daughter, could pay the fine. The demands of justice would then be satisfied. The same principle applies to all mankind. If someone loved us enough to intervene on our behalf, and suffer the consequences of our violating the law, they could also satisfy the demands of justice on our behalf.

The laws of sociality in the universe are not based on any monetary system—so how can the demands of justice be fulfilled by another person on our behalf?

The person satisfying the demands of justice on our behalf must be seriously motivated by love or they would not do it. In order for them to satisfy the demands of justice on our behalf, the person must do the following:

- Understand completely and comprehend perfectly the violation of the law that was committed. The judge would obviously want the party willing to intervene on our behalf to understand the punishment they were willing to take upon themselves. If the person fulfilling the demands of justice on our behalf did not fully understand the violations, they would not know what was necessary to satisfy the demands of justice.

- Be willing to suffer the punishment decreed by the demands of justice for violating the law such as mental anguish, heartache, and despair, which is the punishment for violating the laws of sociality.

No one would want to do anything like the above for us unless they had a tremendous love for us. If it was for just one violation of the law, it would be one thing, but to do so for numerous violations is almost incomprehensible. It is hard to think that anyone would want to suffer so much for another person. Why not let them suffer for their own violations of the law? A person's love for us would have to transcend our understanding. Such a person would undoubtedly limit such action to those persons who would really appreciate it and would want to alter their behavior to conform to all the laws.

There is such a person whom God has arranged for to fulfill the demands of justice on our behalf. He is Jesus Christ. We would be wise to follow His procedure for obtaining mercy. If we do not follow His procedures, we must fulfill the demands of justice all by ourselves. It is like buying insurance. If we buy insurance by living the laws of sociality that God and Christ have set forth, we are covered and will not suffer the demands of justice. If we do not, we will suffer the demands of justice. Living by the laws of sociality, as taught by Jesus Christ, is good insurance against suffering the demands of justice. It is wise to pay the premium for mercy by abiding by all of His teachings.

One of Christ's requirements before He will grant us mercy is to be immersed in water to symbolize His burial in the tomb for three days, and arising again. It is very important that we do this. Every organization has some requirement in order to join it. Jesus Christ also requires that this be done as a symbol of our desire to change our lives and follow his teachings. Without doing so, it is a sign of rebellion and He will not grant us mercy. It is necessary for all of us to do our homework and find who has the authority from Jesus Christ to perform this function. We must ask God for direction in this matter.

Conclusion

The laws of physics, or natural laws, are rigid and grant no mercy if violated. It is the same with the laws of sociality, except that we may escape the consequences of violating the laws of sociality if we adhere to all of the requirements established by Jesus Christ who is the only one who even claims that He has the ability to fulfill the demands of justice so God will grant us mercy. We should play it safe and conform to all His requirements to obtain mercy as stipulated by Him. It is simply good insurance and *will do us no harm*. It will be hard for us to bear, and we will be miserable if we do not because we have all violated the laws of sociality at some time or another. We will have to satisfy the demands of justice all by ourselves.

Chapter 14:

Mankind's Future

The Easy Way

If we desire to follow the easy way, we will diligently seek to learn and continually change our ways to conform to the laws of sociality and the instructions given to us by our God. This allows us to be granted mercy and avoid the excruciating pain and suffering imposed by the demands of justice when we do not live to merit mercy.

Psychologists know that our moral behavior determines what we believe in. Only when we want to change our moral behavior will we change our beliefs.

The Hard Way

The hard way to live is to violate the laws of nature or the laws of sociality. If we desire to learn and obey the laws of nature and the laws of sociality, our future can be glorious beyond description. If we do not obey these laws, our future will be full of pain, suffering, and despair until we learn to obey all the laws. *We learn obedience by the things we suffer.* God does not want us to be unhappy and suffer forever, but we will always be unhappy and suffer unless we change and conform to all the laws.

Conclusion

We reach our final state of existence the easy way or the hard way. The hard way, if we do not live in accordance with all the laws and, therefore, must experience suffering to change, or the easy way if we are granted mercy and are able to change our behavior without suffering. Our final state can be glorious beyond our comprehension because of the love God has for us. However, it is logical that some will attain greater happiness because they have been more diligent in obeying all the laws. The following chart has been prepared showing mankind's future for those becoming obedient to natural and social laws.

The following chart has been prepared showing mankind's future for those obedient to natural and social laws.

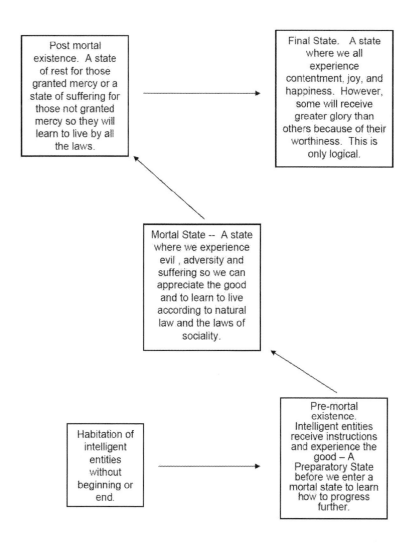

**The Evolution of Man
And
His Destiny**

Post mortal existence. A state of rest for those granted mercy or a state of suffering for those not granted mercy so they will learn to live by all the laws.

Final State. A state where we all experience contentment, joy, and happiness. However, some will receive greater glory than others because of their worthiness. This is only logical.

Mortal State -- A state where we experience evil , adversity and suffering so we can appreciate the good and to learn to live according to natural law and the laws of sociality.

Habitation of intelligent entities without beginning or end.

Pre-mortal existence. Intelligent entities receive instructions and experience the good – A Preparatory State before we enter a mortal state to learn how to progress further.

Chapter 15:

How Can We Know for Sure?

Epistemologists[4] generally agree that there are four ways to know something. You can know from the testimony of others, by reason, by experience, and by intuition or feeling. We shall examine each of these ways of knowing and determine how we can know if the explanations in this book are true. In summary, the ways of knowing listed below can simply be summed up as the "scientific method" for establishing intangible truths.

1. **Testimony of others.** We learn from others. Sometimes we do not interpret what people say correctly, which causes us to draw wrong conclusions, or to form incorrect paradigms concerning various matters. Sometimes others outright lie to us. Nevertheless, most of our learning comes from the testimony of others. Testimonies of one person can be weighed against the testimonies of others to help us better understand the truth. The greater the number of testimonies concerning a matter, the more likely the truth, but all testimonies should be questioned as they could all be wrong and we could be deceived. We must remember that it is important to know *what* is right—not *who* is right.

2. **Reason.** We all have reasoned things out in our minds only to find out later that our reasoning was faulty. We can reason incorrectly when doing mathematics or when assessing any situation. We cannot always rely on our reasoning alone

and must combine our reasoning with the other ways of knowing before a matter can be considered to be true.

3. **Experience.** Most all of us have had experiences where our interpretation differs from the interpretation of another person. This is evident in the courtroom when two witnesses are called to testify. One witness may say one thing and another witness something else. We can often draw false conclusions from our experiences. We cannot rely entirely on our experience, but if we combine our experiences with the other ways of knowing, we can be more assured that we have arrived at the truth. Knowledge can also come from conducting experiments in laboratories—the results of which can consistently be replicated by others.

4. **Intuition, or feelings.** Intuition can better be described as a feeling. If we feel really good about a matter, we can feel more confident that our conclusions are correct—but it must conform to the other ways of knowing, including private confirmation from God himself. We can receive private confirmation from God by applying the basics of the scientific method to ideas as shown below.

Using the Basics of the Scientific Method on Ideas

The fastest way to learn the truth about any philosophical, ideological, or religious idea is to experiment with the idea. There is a different way that we must conduct experiments with ideas to ascertain their truthfulness, which is compatible with and conforms to the scientific method. In actuality, the steps we must take are basically the same steps we take when conducting scientific experiments. The steps are as follows:

Desire: We must have a sincere desire to know the truth, whether it is a scientific, philosophical, ideological, or religious problem. If we do not desire to know, we will obviously never put forth the effort to know.

Research: We must diligently research and study ideas, insert them into the crucible of our mind, and make sure they conform to the ways of knowing. We can then draw conclusions that must be tested further.

Belief: We must believe that we can actually find out if the ideas we are exploring are true or not.

Seek Private Confirmation from God to See If Our Conclusions Are Correct

Once we have arrived at a conclusion, we must seek confirmation from God that our conclusion is correct. The following shows how this is done privately.

How to Receive Private Confirmation

Experiments have been conducted to see if God will confirm or reject conclusions. Some people are close minded and think they already know the answers. They feel it is demeaning and unscientific to ask God. If we humbly ask God, He will confirm or reject our conclusion, providing we have done our homework, and if we diligently seek answers and ask in the right way. Experiments concerning this matter have proven that asking God actually works. The process is like other scientific processes. We must follow certain procedures to receive answers and recognize when answers have been received. Here is the step-by-step process for receiving answers from God.

1. *We must pray in private. We must realize that we are never too evil or unworthy to pray.* No matter how evil or unworthy we feel, the Lord wants to help us—and will help

us—if we sincerely want him to. He will not help us if we are not sincere or do not think we will receive an answer.

> He said "Ask, and it shall be given unto you; seek, and ye shall find; knock and it shall be opened unto you: *For every one that asketh, receiveth;* and he that seeketh findeth; and to him that knocketh it shall be opened. Or what man is there of you, whom if his son ask bread, will he give him a stone? Or if he ask a fish, will he give him a serpent? If ye then, being evil, know how to give good gifts unto your children, how much more shall your Father which is in heaven give good things to them that ask him?" (Matthew 7:7-11; italics added)

We cannot simply ask and expect an answer without seeking diligently and putting forth the proper effort to receive an answer. Seeking is a vital requirement. The following steps are of prime importance and show what we must do to receive answers.

2. **Study.** We must be persistent and study any issue in our mind and form our own conclusions before answers will come. The Lord will help us similar to the way we help our children. He will not do our homework for us anymore than we should do homework for our children in school. Children would not learn properly if we did. The principle is the same. The Lord will simply not form conclusions for us. If He did, we would not grow and progress. We must study things in our mind, form our own conclusions, and then ask the Lord to confirm or reject our conclusions. If not, we will not grow and learn what we need to know. We must be as teachable as a little child. Once we become teachable, we can receive answers to our prayers. If you would like to start doing homework, a good place to start would be to read the first four books of the New Testament.

3. **Understanding how prayers are answered.** The Lord expects us to study things in our mind and form a conclusion. We must do our homework and formulate our own answers first. With proper due diligence on our part, we can. The Lord will then answer us in various ways and at various times. We must unwaveringly pursue the answers we are seeking. We can receive an answer all at once, but mostly answers come a little at a time, and seldom at the same time we are asking. He will answer us at a time we will be the most receptive—a time when we will not be stubborn and will accept changes in our thinking. Answers usually come when we have found quiet time to think and meditate privately. The most common way we receive answers to prayers are as follows:

d. **Enlightening ideas.** Ideas will suddenly come into our mind. These ideas become pieces of the whole that makes everything make sense. These ideas can be just what we need. They can also lead to other ideas that enlighten and expand our understanding. When this happens, we should acknowledge that the Lord is helping us. Acknowledgment brings further enlightenment.

e. **Gentle promptings.** We can receive gentle promptings that nudge us to act. Such promptings are given to assist us in our quest for truth. They should be acted upon.

f. **Feelings of peace.** When we have done all we can do, and presented our conclusions before the Lord to confirm or reject them, the Lord will tell us in our mind and in our heart whether our conclusions and decisions are correct. A feeling of peace, love, and contentment will come over us. We will have peace of mind and joy in knowing that we have arrived at a truth. If our conclusions are not correct, we will have a feeling of confusion come over us and we will not feel peace, joy, or contentment. We will have the feeling that we must search further and that our conclusions are not right. We will feel in our mind and in our heart that we have not arrived at the right conclusion.

Answers to prayers are felt more than they are heard. We must realize that it is difficult to feel an answer if we do not resolve to live in accordance with all laws. An answer is like a delicious peach to be savored. We cannot savor fully a delicious peach if we have a sin like a hot pepper in our mouth. We must resolve to get rid of the hot pepper before we can savor the delicious peach. Our God will help us get rid of our unsavory actions if we want Him to and sincerely seek His help in doing so. Answers will then be more easily comprehended—even though the Lord answers all sincere prayers if we carefully sort out the answer.

To summarize, we can know for certain about a matter if we have the desire, are persistent with our studies, and attempt to live as we should. If we conduct experiments concerning prayer as we explained above, we will find that such experiments produce results just as any experiment in science produces results. We must not try to manipulate the answer to fit our desires. We must accept the answer—no matter what the consequences may be—and accept enlightenment with thankfulness. It may not be the answer that we desire or even expect, but it will be what is expedient for us.

Conclusion

Traditions and the opinions of others often keep us from discovering the real truth. Remember that it is not who is right, but what is right. Truth is felt more than it is heard—and usually only after we sincerely and diligently do our homework. We must form our own conclusions and ask the Lord if our conclusions are correct because the *Lord will not do our homework for us.* If our conclusions are not correct, we will feel confused about the matter and realize that we must search further. If our conclusions are correct, we will have a feeling of peace, love, and contentment come over us. We will have peace of mind—and *know for sure.* We will be filled with happiness and joy and be content.

We can understand the whole picture of where we came from, why we are here, and what we can expect in the future if we simply follow the procedures outlined by the Lord for obtaining light and knowledge as explained above.

Chapter 16:

Logic, Science, and God—How It All Fits Together

Fitting logic, science, and God together is like putting together a jigsaw puzzle. In this chapter, we will review each of the previous chapters to see how they fit together and make a logical whole picture.

Chapter 1: *The Origin of Man*

Newton's third law of physics is true and shows that nothing can be made without things that act (Intelligent Entities) to move upon matter. Intelligent Entities can act and have always existed. It has been shown that nothing happens by chance; and if man's intelligence was made from scratch, we would have to come to two conclusions as shown below:

1. **Men would be robots.** Man would be robots and could only act as they were programmed or *made* to act.

2. **Man would have no need for ethical teachings.** It would be unjust and wrong to punish anyone if we were made from scratch. We would only be acting according to how we were made or programmed to act. Man is responsible for his own actions and needs ethical teaching to learn how to live happily and in harmony with other Intelligent Entities.

    The fact that our intelligence has always existed is essential to understand and to show how all concepts fit together. It is the foundation to comprehending how all things complement each other. *It fits as the keystone of the puzzle.*

Chapter 2: *Two Categories of Laws Governing the Universe*

No one can rationally dispute that we must learn and obey the two categories of laws governing the universe—natural laws and the laws of sociality. We must obey these laws in order to evolve into a higher state of existence where knowledge, joy, and happiness abound—a state much higher than we are presently in. The requirement to obey all laws fits as part of the puzzle showing that all concepts fit together.

Chapter 3: *Is There a Need for a God?*

It fits to understand there must be an Intelligent Entity willing to assist us in our evolution toward a higher state of existence. It is also imperative to understand that we need a God to assist in dispensing justice in the universe so we can live in peace.

Chapter 4: *Darwin's Contributions*

Darwin was right concerning two of his basic concepts, namely that the earth is much older than seven days or even seven thousand years, and survival of the fittest, or natural selection, assists in preserving the species. These concepts cannot logically be construed to mean that man or animals evolved by chance. We have shown that this cannot happen. Darwin did discover some truths, but there is much more to be discovered. The concepts referred to above do not conflict with logic or science—and easily fit together with other concepts explained herein.

Chapter 5: *Evolution—True or False? Dogma versus Logic and Science*

Correct reasoning using sound deductive logic is essential to arriving at the truth. We can logically conclude that evolution occurs—but evolution does not occur by chance as creations do not occur by chance. It takes a thing to act (an Intelligent Entity) to cause creation to occur. Evolution occurs, but defining evolution correctly and dispelling illogical dogma concerning evolution is necessary to show how everything fits together. We must understand that the belief that man was created by chance is more related to religion than to science.

Chapter 6: *Lessons from a Bluebird*

The bluebird thought that he knew it all and kept doing the same thing over and over again. It fits that we must not be guilty of doing the same wrong thing over and over again or we will not evolve into a higher state.

Chapter 7: *Learning Is Necessary to Progress and Be Happy*

It is logical that we cannot progress or evolve into a higher state of happiness without learning. In order to comprehend how everything fits together, we must learn the correct concepts concerning science, God, and the laws of sociality—or we cannot evolve into a higher, happier state. It fits that we must learn and gain knowledge in order to progress.

Chapter 8: *Can We Ever Know All There Is to Know?*

There is not a cap on learning. We can continue learning until we know all things. There are omniscient Intelligent Entities in the universe that control all laws or the universe would be in a constant state of chaos. Knowing this helps us understand how all the concepts in this book fit together.

Chapter 9: *Is the Bible Compatible with Science?*

The Bible's teachings concerning the laws of sociality are logical and benefit mankind. The Bible's ethical teachings do not conflict with science. It fits that it is necessary for us to learn and follow the Bible's ethical teachings if we are to be content and happy.

Chapter 10: *What Does God Look Like?*

We do know what God looks like. He has told us plainly that we are made in his image, according to the Bible. If we are made in God's image, He must have an image like ours—a manlike image. Understanding that God is manlike in form fits with the concept that we—as men and women—can also evolve over time to where we have knowledge and other attributes like Him. It is difficult to visualize anything different that we could worship.

Chapter 11: *What Motivates God and Other Intelligent Entities to Help Us?*

God will guide us and help us because He loves us as parents do children. Loving and assisting others brings happiness. It is the same with God. Guiding us with our progression brings him happiness. It fits that we must also possess love toward other Intelligent Entities in order to evolve into a higher state of existence. It fits that God is motivated to assist us because He loves us.

Chapter 12: *The Necessity of Experiencing Adversity, Death, Sorrow, Pain and Suffering*

It is absolutely necessary for us to experience death, sorrow, adversity, pain, and suffering in order to appreciate the absence of such things in our lives and to have empathy for those who experience such. It fits to know that it is an essential part of our learning and understanding.

Chapter 13: *How God Administers Justice and Still Grants Mercy*

If we are not granted mercy, we must suffer the penalties ourselves before we can progress. There is only one man in all history who has claimed to be the judge that can grant mercy. He is Jesus Christ. We can only progress when we obey laws. Justice must prevail and the penalties for violating laws must be enforced to preserve harmony and to prevent chaos in the universe. Penalties must be enforced—whether we pay the penalties ourselves or someone else pays them. We must understand that Jesus Christ was called upon by God to suffer the consequences of all mankind's disobedience to law, and therefore became authorized to grant mercy to those willing to be obedient to the laws. He fulfilled the law of justice on our behalf by suffering in our place when we broke the laws of sociality. Therefore, God can administer justice and still get mercy. It fits that we must understand and abide by this principle in order to be granted mercy and avoid suffering ourselves.

Chapter 14: *Mankind's Future*

We must conclude that mankind's future is marvelous—way beyond our comprehension—because of the love our God has for us. However, some will attain a greater glory because they have been more diligent in obeying the laws of sociality.

Chapter 15: *How Can We Know for Sure?*

We can know for sure if a concept is true if we sincerely do our homework—and *then* ask God if it is true. God will tell us in our heart and in our mind if it is true or not. If it is true, He will enlighten our understanding and instill in us a feeling of warmth and contentment. We become truly happy and thankful when we discover the truth. It fits that we must do this to understand our origin, why we are on this earth, and where we go when we leave this earth.

Chapter 16: *Logic, God, Science, and God—How It All Fits Together.*

The general concepts in this book fit together to assist us in understanding the whole picture concerning our origin, why we are here on this earth, and what we can expect when we leave this earth.

Chapter 17:

The Challenge

The reader is challenged to find any fault with the logic contained in this book. There is a saying which is as follows:

- If you have facts, talk facts.
- If you do not have facts, talk authority.
- If you do not have authority, talk loud and make fun of it.

If anyone wishes to logically discuss the concepts of this book, feel free to email us at logicscienceandgod@gmail.com. Please avoid talking authority, loud talk, or trying to reduce the concepts contained herein to an absurdum without using sound logic to do so.

Notes

[1] Sir Isaac Newton, *Philosophiæ Naturalis Principia Mathematica*, 1687.

[2] Charles Darwin, *The Works of Charles Darwin, Volume 16: The Origin of Species*, 1876.

[3] *The Holy Bible, King James Version*, University Press, Cambridge, 1979.

[4] Wm. Pepperell. Montague, *The Ways of Knowing or the Methods of Philosophy*, 1925.